Signs of the End Times.

Key Events To Watch.

ERIKA GREY

Pedante Press

Short Book Series

001

Copyright © 2020 Erika Grey

All rights reserved.

Special Thanks to Jerri O'Roke who proofread and edited this work.

ISBN: 978-1-940844-13-8

DEDICATION

To my father who made this work possible.

CONTENTS

	Acknowledgments	i
1	Parable of the Fig Tree	1
2	Signs in Nature	7
3	Social Signs-Violence & Immorality	10
4	Geopolitical Signs	17
5	Israel	21
6	Ezekiel 38-39 War	23
7	The Revived Roman Empire	26
8	The US and Bible Prophecy	29
9	Technology	31
10	Globalization and More	34

www.erikagrey.com

For Bible Prophecy news and analysis and more books visit my website. For Bible Prophecy Updates on video subscribe to my YouTube channel Prophecy Talk with Erika Grey.

1 PARABLE OF THE FIG TREE

Nearly one-third of Biblical passages are prophetic. Those dealing with past events have been fulfilled with astounding accuracy. The forecasts dealing with the Tribulation remain open to fulfillment. The series of predictions that Christians term 'signs of the end times' are unfolding as you read these pages.

Many Bible verses provide insight into the signs of the end times. These comprise entire passages and verses. They number about ten. Many more dot the pages of Scripture. Yet these ten make up the core passages. They are as follows:

Matthew 24

Mark 13
Luke 21
2 Timothy 3:1-5
2 Peter 3
1Timothy 4:1-2
Revelation 13
Daniel 12:4
Revelation 13:18
Revelation 17

The above passages signs overlap with events that will precede the Tribulation—to those that occur during it.

The Tribulation

God unleashes the judgments detailed in the Revelation during the Tribulation. This is the time frame when these will occur. The Bible specifies a seven-year duration. These judgments lead to the battle of Armageddon and the end of the World. The Tribulation divides into two halves. Scholars named the second half "the Great Tribulation" because during this period, the angels release the worst of the Revelation plagues. Jesus and one of the 24 Elders in the Revelation also referred to the days as "the Great Tribulation."

The Parable of the Fig Tree

Three of the Gospels record the Parable of the Fig Tree teaching by Jesus: Matthew 24:32-35, Mark 13:28-31, and Luke 21:29-33 relay various versions.

The Parable of the Fig Tree references appear in the signs of the end time passages. Think of the tree as depicting unfolding events. These extend into the next branch with smaller limbs protruding.

The signs exhibit a fractal pattern—one leads to the next. We see this in the fig tree example. At the end its fruit or buds appear. This illustrates the time frame referred to as the "end times." All Christians agree we are living in the end times; however, many teachers can't identify the fruit. Additionally, they do not understand the events that led to the current times or what is coming next.

Misreading the Tree

The passage in Luke 21:29-31 reads:

Then He spoke to them a parable: "Look at the fig tree, and all the trees. When they are already budding, you see and know for yourselves that summer is now near. So you also, when you see these things happening, know that the kingdom of God is near."

The old expression, "You're barking up the wrong tree" describes many of today's prophecy teachers. As a result, the Bible classifies their teachings as "cunningly devised fables." Unfortunately, the followers of these teachers believe in stone walls that lead nowhere in the unfolding of the prophetic events.

Knowing the Fig Tree–What it is Not

The fig tree must align with history. Remember that the apostles referred to their days as the last days. Therefore, all historical events from the death and resurrection of the Lord Jesus Christ make up the tree. Events such as the Templars protecting Jerusalem in the Middle Ages to the Westphalia Treaty of 1648 are branches. The Monarchies and their end by the French Revolution depicts another. Revelation 17 and 18 describes the Whore of Babylon and her judgement. These occur, in part, as a result of the actions that began with the Roman Empire in the age of the apostles, to the rule of the Papacy in the Holy Roman Empire.

Buds and Branches on the Fig Tree

The birth of the nation-state, and the rapid growth of them in the 1800's and 1900's, lead to the rebirth of the nation of Israel. Almost simultaneously, the formation of the EU began, which would also become a key end time prophetic development. The EU will launch the Antichrist, who then signs a treaty with Israel. This marks the beginning event of the Tribulation. If World War I did not happen, world leaders would not have signed the treaty at Versailles. This led to World War II. These wars birthed the nation of Israel and the European Union.

Trees that are not the Fig Tree

Conspiracy theories, along with those that only look at the latest news headlines, are not the fig tree. Many false teachings exist in end time prophecy. Conspiracy theories of any sort or variety top the list. The Islam as the Beast of Revelation teaching capitalized on all the ISIS Caliphate headlines. This situation is past, and the theory has died down.

I have sited the geopolitical errors here; but in deciphering other signs, errors exist as well. You will understand this further as you read on.

2 SIGNS IN NATURE

End time signs fall into sections. We can also list the end time verses into both categories and subcategories. They are as follows:

Nature

We derive these from Matthew 24:7, which states, "And there will be famines, pestilences, and earthquakes in various places." Mark 13:8 reads; "And there will be earthquakes in various places, and there will be famines and troubles." The word for troubles means disturbances, commotions, and tumults. Luke 21:11 predicts, "And there will be great earthquakes in various places, and famines and pestilences; and there will be fearful sights and great signs from heaven."

Nature has several subcategories:

Extreme weather Tornadoes, floods, droughts, typhoons, hurricanes, heat waves, polar vortexes, record hail and snow fall. Also, brush fires and any record-breaking weather event.

Decline of the ecosystem These erosions occur from the extreme weather. A prime example is the melting of the polar ice caps.

Unusual occurrences in nature These events include large numbers of animals suddenly dying and large sinkholes appearing out of nowhere.

Earthquakes

While earthquakes need no explanation, teachers over report them in end time news. Some report on every earthquake that occurs. In fact, a certain number of earthquakes are expected each year. Only the large earthquakes that break records or occur in unusual places should be considered an end time sign.

Pestilences

The word in the Greek is plural and is used twice in the New Testament. It is the only place in Scripture we see pestilences used in plural. The word defines as both a plague of pests or insects or rodents. The second definition includes illnesses or viruses; e.g., SARS, Ebola, Zika Virus and COVID-19.

Famines

Jesus predicted famines. These would occur in addition to the great famine predicted in Revelation 6. It has become evident that extreme weather will produce some of these. In addition, the plagues of pests such as locusts and the erosion of the ecosystem will usher in more. All of this will lead to the great famine of Revelation 6 that will most likely be kicked off by an event wrought by God's hand of judgement.

3 SOCIAL SIGNS-VIOLENCE

Daniel 8:23 predicts that the end of the world events will occur "when the transgressors are come to the full."

According to the Hebrew word pasha, transgressors, in part, defines as "when the number of their sins is completed." This means men and women will commit every imaginable and wicked sin. Jesus predicts and confirms in Matthew 24:12; "lawlessness will abound."

Increased Violence In the Days of Noah

Jesus provided more specifics. He compared the days before His coming to the era of Noah and Lot (Matt. 24:37, Luke 17:26). As in the days of Noah, violence becomes an epidemic (Gen. 6:11-12).

Lawless

Jesus said the days would be lawless. Lawlessness characterized the days of Lot when men called good evil and evil good.

Nation Will Rise Against Nation

With the increased violence, people will not get along; neither will nations. We will see more conflicts between nations, and this means more wars. In addition, we will witness more riots, commotions and conflicts. People will not get along in government, churches, businesses and families.

2 Timothy 3:1-5 Perilous Times

The Bible describes the last days as perilous because of the heartless actions of others. 2 Timothy 3:1-5 sums them up perfectly. The passage reads:

"But know this, that in the last days perilous times will come: For men will be lovers of themselves, lovers of money, boasters, proud, blasphemers, disobedient to parents, unthankful, unholy, unloving, unforgiving, slanderers, without self-control, brutal, despisers of good, traitors, headstrong, haughty, lovers of pleasure rather than lovers of God, having a form of godliness but denying its power. And from such people turn away!"

2 Timothy Gives Us Specifics

Within the 2 Timothy list we can isolate other social maladies. Many of these expand on Jesus's warning and description of increased violence and sexual immorality. Some are a symptom of Daniel 8:23, i.e. the sinners coming to the full. The following is the list broken down.

Lovers of themselves - High divorce rate, among many other sins as one seeks to put themselves first.

Lovers of money - Increase in crimes of greed, scams, swindling, preying on other's vulnerabilities to get their money, stealing, family members stealing from family members.

Boasters-Proud-Blasphemers-disobedient to parents-unthankful-unholy-unloving-

unforgiving-slanderers - Entitlement, no regard for God or Jesus or for others. Full of hate, resentment, bitterness, vengeful, and backbiting. Lying about others to make them look bad. Also, people become both vile and evil. From unloving we see an increase in all kinds of horrific child and animal abuse.

Without self-control, brutal, despisers of good - Without self-control is frightening. This means that men and women will not control any of their excesses or deviant appetites. The next describes many of the crimes we now see. It states that they will be brutal. We see this brutality and lack of self-control in many areas; ISIS provided a classic example. It includes anything from increases of road rage, to brutal rapes of children, to war crimes. These are the shocking stories that fill the airwaves today. There are people who literally have no mercy or empathy for the suffering of others. In addition, they are capable of inflicting unimaginable acts of violence. They are summed up in people becoming "despisers of good."

Betrayals

2 Timothy also records, **"traitors, headstrong, haughty."** Jesus warned of betrayals in the Gospels. These would characterize the Tribulation period. Not only are these betrayals forewarned of in the Gospels, but also in Micah 7.

While these result from family members turning in each other for not taking the mark of the beast during the Tribulation, they also describe behavior in the end times. We see the rise of betrayals in relationships evidenced by infidelities to many other areas.

"Headstrong" means that no one will talk these individuals out of their evil deeds. In addition, haughty or proud are the attitudes of those who commit these horrific acts. "Haughty" characterizes a superior attitude of those who feel they can do anything that they want no matter who it harms.

Lovers of Pleasure-Addictions

2 Timothy concludes with the list of social ills, "lovers of pleasure rather than lovers of God, having a form of godliness but denying its power."

Addiction clearly falls under the lover of pleasure category. From overeating to drug and alcohol abuse, all are clearly on the increase. This description also includes obesity, which is gluttony, to drug overdoses and porn and sex addiction.

Their pleasures take precedence over God. Finally, all the above can have a form of godliness but deny its power.

As Was the Time of Lot: Sexual Immorality

In the Gospels, Jesus predicted that along with the end times being like the days of Noah, they will also mirror Lot's day. Lot lived in Sodom and Gomorrah.

God destroyed the cities of Sodom and Gomorrah by raining fire and brimstone on them. These cities were renowned for open homosexuality. Young boys accompanied men and engaged in homosexual and violent activities.

Sodomites apprehended and raped strange men and dealt violently with anyone who tried to stop them (Gen. 19). These peoples had a distorted sense of right and wrong and were lawless. They also exhibit the traits found in 2 Timothy 3:1-5.

Pedophilia

While Sodom and Gomorrah was known for open sexuality, it was also a place of pedophilia. The fact that the Scripture mentions young boys accompanying the men relays this. Joel 3:3, which describes the soldiers in the end times who lay siege to Israel, confirms this.

The verse states: "They have cast lots for my people; have given a boy in exchange for a harlot, and sold a girl for wine, that they might drink." During the Tribulation, soldiers sell children for sexual purposes for as little as a bottle of wine. Men will use boys as prostitutes. These acts describe the level of depravity of the end times: signs which we see unfolding today.

Birth Pangs

Finally, it must be noted that Jesus compared the end time signs to birth pangs. He stated in Matthew 24:8, "These would be the beginning of sorrows." What this means is that all the above signs would occur with great intensity and frequency as we move closer to the start of the Tribulation.

4 GEOPOLITICAL SIGNS

These signs are what we expect to see in geopolitics, such as developments within the leading nations mentioned in prophecy.

The Events of the Tribulation Provide Other Signs

We can speculate on geopolitical signs based on the events that will occur during the Tribulation. While there are many, this work cites the key events.

The Tribulation begins when a peace treaty is signed on behalf of the Antichrist guaranteeing the nation of Israel peace. In the middle of the seven-year Tribulation, the Antichrist breaks the treaty. He goes into the Holy of Holies in the Third Jewish Temple and sets up the abomination of desolation. Afterward, he and the False Prophet initiate the mark of the beast.

This mark will allow those who take it to buy and sell. Those who do not take the mark will be martyred. These predictions are primarily found in the book of Revelation and Daniel.

False Teachings

Geopolitical prophetic analysis comprises the greatest area of errors in end time prophecy. The reason is that many people who have no in-depth knowledge of either the Scriptures or of world affairs set up websites and establish themselves as watchmen. They end up a ready tool of Satan to spread misinformation rather than truth.

It is for this reason conspiracy theories reign in Evangelical circles when they have no place being there. These groups have formed a cult within the Christian community: The New World Order Cult. Other teachers theorize and make up scenarios from news headlines.

Areas with Greatest Errors

The areas with the greatest errors revolve around the final world empire depicted in the book of Daniel and the Revelation. This empire launches the Antichrist. Some claim these prophecies in Daniel were fulfilled.

Main Biblical References for Geopolitical Signs

While there are many forecasts relating to the end times geopolitical framework, the main ones are derived from the book of Daniel and the Revelation. It is astounding how many details are provided in these two books. Yet, there are also many more supporting Scriptures throughout the entire Bible.

The Differing views on the Geopolitical Signs

Along with those who say the Daniel prophecies were already fulfilled are those who teach other lies. One such lie is the Islamic nations will comprise the final world empire. The favored fable is that the final world empire comes about via a conspiracy. In addition, other false teachers identify the Beast of

Revelation as the United States and that the US reigns as Babylon.

So, you may ask, with so many different views on the geopolitical signs, why read further? I ask that you do so because I have written books and put in a great deal of time not only in expounding upon the prophetic forecasts, but also regularly consulting key sources in world affairs. I have interviewed policy makers. I have also written for a secular publication in this area. Within these pages you are getting real analysis.

5 ISRAEL

Geopolitical Signs

Geopolitical signs are those expected to be seen occurring within the leading nations that are mentioned in prophecy; the first and foremost is Israel. All prophecy centers around the nation of Israel.

The Tribulation begins when a peace treaty is signed on behalf of the Antichrist guaranteeing the nation of Israel's peace. In the middle of the seven-year Tribulation, the Antichrist breaks the peace. He goes into the Holy of Holies in the Jewish Third Temple and sets up the abomination of desolation. Simultaneously, he lays siege to Israel and breaks the covenant.

Bible Prophecy Centers on Israel

All Bible Prophecy centers around Israel. We live in the Age of Grace, which ends when the Tribulation begins. When Israel became a nation in 1948, this was major news for prophecy watchers. The continuous conflict Israel has with the Palestinians and its neighbors sets the stage for a future peace treaty that will guarantee the nation's peace and begin the Tribulation.

Jews Return To Israel

With the fall of the Berlin wall in 1990, Jews from behind the iron curtain were able to return to their own land. In addition, immigration laws in the US at the time made Israel the only destination for many Jews giving them no choice but to return to Israel.

Israel Central in World Affairs

The prophet Jeremiah predicted 70 weeks of captivity for Israel. All years have been fulfilled except the final seven. Thus, it is no coincidence that Israel and its conflicts are now central in world affairs.

Signs of the End Times: Key Events to Watch

6 EZEKIEL 38-39 WAR

The Ezekiel 38 -39 war is basically a coalition force spearheaded by Russia and Middle Eastern nations. It is divinely defeated by God Himself. A major earthquake will occur along with other catastrophic events in nature. This will defeat the army. This event will lay the path for the Antichrist's peace treaty. In addition, most likely the Al-Aqsa Mosque, Islam's third holiest site will get destroyed by the great earthquake predicted. This will make way for the building of the Third Temple.

The Third Temple

In Bible Prophecy, Christians—other than preterists—agree that the Third Jewish Temple will be rebuilt. The reason: many prophetic forecasts occur within and around it.

Jesus forecasts the abomination of desolation in the gospels. There are also supporting references in the books of Daniel and Revelation. He also warns of the siege of Jerusalem. This occurs after the abomination of desolation.

When I began my first book in 1989, the desire to build the Third Temple just came into the fore. In 1987, the Temple Institute was founded. Today, the plans are in place for the construction of the third temple. The animals are being raised. The Temple Institute celebrated the birth of an appropriate red heifer. Many of the ritual items used in the temple have been made. The altar is finished. Finally, a sacrifice took place outside of the temple area but as close as possible to it. All of this as it unfolded are key end time signs.

Ezekiel 38-39 War Unfolding

Since it is speculated that the Ezekiel 38-39 war can be responsible for both the Treaty and the Third Temple, its development fits with end time signs.

These signs include the following: Russia forming relations with Iran, Iran's spoken desire to annihilate Israel, Russia's deepening of relations with Turkey and parts of Africa. In addition, Turkey's move away from the European Union is a sign.

Turkey has applied for EU membership. The EU's refusal to let Turkey join due to its policies fits the forecast. We would not expect to see Turkey become an EU member since it is predicted to be part of this alliance.

Finally, lending to the fulfillment is the first discovery of gas in Israel in 1999. Several years later they found more. The reason this is significant is because the Ezekiel 38 passage specifies that the cause for the attack is to take a spoil.

7 THE REVIVED ROMAN EMPIRE

The EU and Bible Prophecy

The revived Roman Empire is key in Bible prophecy because it launches the Antichrist who then signs the peace treaty with Israel. This is the beginning of the Tribulation.

As I have stated earlier concerning the geopolitical errors, the identity of the Beast of Revelation is another major area of disagreement. The many forecasts found throughout the book of Daniel, the Revelation, and other Scriptures clearly support the interpretation that the revived Roman Empire is the Beast of Revelation.

In all of my books, articles and videos that relate to the European Union, I show unfolding sign after sign. The European Union matches up with the prophetic forecasts on so many levels; it is undeniably the final world empire.

Many EU decisions and moves forward are often reported on as signs of the times. Therefore, the EU and Bible Prophecy become a major area of unfolding prophecy news.

Religion's Role

Revelation 17 and 18 depict the Whore of Babylon—she rides the Beast. This means she is influential in the final world empire's formation.

There are many cliché's in Bible Prophecy, and some are too specific, such as one world religion. These individuals follow the ecumenical movement and report on it. They also erroneously teach that there will be a one world religion.

I do not teach a one world religion. Rather, as the passage specifies, I show the Catholic churches' influence in the formation of the

European Union. It is clear in the passage that, during the Tribulation, the Antichrist—and his ten kings—destroy the Whore and do not tolerate any form of religion. Thus, a one world religion along with the Beast is ignoring important Scriptures.

The Ten King Federation

The ten king federation forecast mentioned in both the books of Daniel and the Revelation are key Tribulation prophecies. Still, it is another area that is butchered by Bible Prophecy wannabe forecasters who do not have a clue as to how world affairs work.

Fiction and fables reign in this area. What has yet to unfold is literally made up. Theories that have no basis in foreign policy are taught as unfolding fulfillment.

The Ten King Federation is Forming

The Bible depicts the EU in its final powerful form. There is a ten-nation federation along with the Antichrist. In my reporting, I tell how the idea of breaking up the European Union into an inner core has been evolving. This lines up with this prophecy. There is also a clause in the EU's recent Lisbon Treaty that paves the way for this inner chamber. All developments in this area are unfolding signs of the end times.

8 THE US & BIBLE PROPHECY

Most prophecy teachers agree that the United States does not have a leading place during the Tribulation. Some wonder if the US is annihilated beforehand. I believe it is the great nation mentioned in Jeremiah 6:22 that is heading to Armageddon alongside the King of the North. It states: Thus says the Lord: "Behold, a people comes from the north country, And a great nation will be raised from the farthest parts of the earth."

In that the US does not have a leading role, we have safely speculated that its great power status will decline. This will occur simultaneously as the EU—or revived Roman Empire—gains power. This especially includes having its own army. In addition, the role of NATO will change and its relevance will diminish. The continued rise of the EU and the demise of the US are unfolding signs.

The US Dollar and Euro

The US dollar is the symbol of US strength and power. The dollar is the world's reserve currency. We know that the dollar will lose this status. In my speculation, based on the forecasts, it will be replaced by the euro. The euro is the currency of the European Union, i.e., the revived Roman empire. Thus, the weakening or fall of the dollar are unfolding end time signs. This also includes any developments of the euro as the world's reserve.

A Day Coming Soon

There is a day coming in the near future when the decline of the US will no longer be reported as a sign of the times. It will have occurred. In addition, the dollar will no longer be the world's reserve. It will have been replaced by the euro. Americans who once enjoyed great prosperity will experience difficult times.

Signs of the End Times: Key Events to Watch

9 TECHNOLOGY

Advances in technology are major end time signs. These are based on Daniel 12:4, which states "But you, Daniel, shut up the words, and seal the book until the time of the end; many shall run to and for, and knowledge shall increase." How far that knowledge will increase is also relayed in the book of Revelation.

Revelation chapters 13 and 14 describe the mark, which is a noncash payment system. The Bible refers to it as the Beast. The Scripture also states that the entire world shall worship the Beast and take the mark. Those who do not take it are killed. It is more than a payment system; by taking the mark, you pay your allegiance to the Antichrist.

The Revelation 13:15-18 states:

He was granted power to give breath to the image of the beast, that the image of the beast should both speak and cause as many as would not worship the image of the beast to be killed. He causes all, both small and great, rich and poor, free and slave, to receive a mark on their right hand or on their foreheads, and that no one may buy or sell except one who has the mark or the name of the beast, or the number of his name.

Here is wisdom. Let him who has understanding calculate the number of the beast, for it is the number of a man: His number is 666.

The Mark of the Beast

Almost all prophecy teachers agree that the mark of the Beast is a technological payment system that will use a type of microchip technology. Thus, when the first chips came on the scene, prophecy teachers reported these as signs of the times. They also relay stories of places that have begun to microchip individuals for various purposes.

In that many teachers identify the mark of the Beast as a cashless payment system, the stories that highlight the elimination of cash in society are reported as another sign.

Other Mark of the Beast Technology

As time has gone on, there have been more developments. These advances can also fit the mark of the beast prediction. In addition, some of these shed light on just how the Antichrist will use technology for his diabolical aims.

Thus, advances in bio implants, brain to brain technology, CRISPR (which is gene editing), robotics, G-6, holograms, digital printing, and quantum computing all qualify as signs of the end times.

10 GLOBALIZATION

With the reference in the Revelation passage to the entire world worshipping the Beast, the globalization of the world has been on the radar of prophecy watchers. The formation of world institutions and developments within them are often reported as a sign of the times. However, herein also lies another area for false teachings.

New World Order

This is one of the biggest catch phrases for those who follow end time signs. It was first stated by former president George Bush Sr. at a podium in 1992. The Bible Prophecy world has used and abused it ever since. Frankly, they have beaten it into the ground. It is the most over used cliché of end time Bible Prophecy. New World Order has found its home in every single Bible Prophecy conspiracy theory. Part of the reason for the phrase's overuse and abuse is just plainly lack of study on the part of the teacher. Conspiracy theories offer an easy way out of studying.

Empire Age

The book of Daniel predicts a history of empires and predicts the final world empire that ushers in the end. Geopolitically we are in a multi-polar world or empire age. The European Union is the final world empire; thus, all references to the age of empires and a multipolar world are another sign.

The final globalization of this world will come about via the Antichrist when he heads the European Union. When it becomes the world's leading superpower, the Antichrist will be able to use the weight of this power to lead the world into global governance. They will have no choice but to conform to EU law, or the EU will not allow their companies to trade in their vast market.

Signs Must Align with Facts

The signs and events leading to the Tribulation are so in place that we can speculate on the next main developments to watch for. But, the signs must be based on accurate facts. God brings prophecy about through the order of events. There is not going to be a supernatural appearing of the Antichrist on the scene. Neither will geopolitical events suddenly snap into place. Nor is there a conspiracy bringing everything about.

When someone teaches a conspiracy theory, they might as well have a loudspeaker and shout, "I don't have the time for the research or the skills so I will just adopt this theory that will seize your emotions." In the meantime, they teach what the Bible refers to as a 'cunningly devised fable.' More importantly, they end up dishonoring the name of Jesus by making the people of the King look like fools in the eyes of the world.

It is one thing to be one for Christ, but another to be caught up in the ridiculous lies that negate the power of our great God and the Lord Jesus Christ.

Be Careful - There is No Standard Within Bible Prophecy News

There is no standard for Bible Prophecy news. Anyone can jump online and begin a website or a YouTube channel. Many so called end time prophecy teachers are not writing books on the topic. Neither do they put in the time for the study. These individuals might do okay teaching on the writings, but only if they stick to Scripture and the basics. They just will not have the time it takes for proper study in the geopolitical realm, along with taking care of members of their church and families.

Know Your Teacher

There is no official accreditation to teach Bible Prophecy news in Evangelical circles. It is up to the student of prophecy to examine their teacher along with their analysis. Look for authored books, articles and first contributions by the teachers to understand the prophetic teachings. Make sure the sources they site are legitimate, not fake news or news aggregates. These are sites that get news from many sources and hand pick articles from their view. Your prophecy teacher should be acting as the aggregate. Finally, make sure you are not on a site that is one of the cults. The authors of some of those sites are not so obvious. Look for a statement of faith or of end time beliefs.

If you prefer, with the information provided in this article, you can do your own digging to see what is unfolding.

A list of news sources

News Wires-Associated Press, Reuters, UPI
Mainstream global Media Outlets in both the EU, US, Israel, Russia, and China, some have more prestige than others such as the
Financial Times over the Wall Street Journal, Euractiv over Politico EU,
Think tanks in both the EU and US and these each have a bias
Foreign policy journals
World Organization publications
Central Bank publications, press releases and speeches
White House Briefing Room
Knesset Press Releases
The Kremlin
The European Commission reports, press releases, audio visual
The European Parliament reports, press releases, speeches from the MEP's

Leading Universities such as London School of Economics, MIT,
Interviews with leaders and notables in their fields
Twitter accounts and Facebook pages of leading politicians
EU Political Party president pages, press releases and speeches

Most Important Resource

In the study of end time prophecy, your most important resource is ALWAYS the Bible. Never has so much information been available at the touch of a mouse. In addition to theologians whose works are online, there are great Bible information sites which provide commentary and explanations of Biblical terms. Most importantly, use a Concordance. This will allow you to do word studies at the click of a mouse.

God Bless you on your journey into learning more about Bible Prophecy. May you be richly blessed as you discover the unfolding signs just as they were predicted in God's Word.

ABOUT THE AUTHOR

Erika Grey, author, Bible scholar, commentator, journalist has been a born again Christian for over 40 years. She has written numerous books on Bible Prophecy and made contributions in helping to decode the more difficult forecasts. She has spoken on numerous radio stations including Coast to Coast and interviewed high level policy makers.

This book is one of a series of short books by Erika Grey intended to be quick reads with important information. Be sure to check out Erika's other titles at www.erikagrey.com.

www.ingramcontent.com/pod-product-compliance
Lightning Source LLC
Chambersburg PA
CBHW020235170426
43201CB00007B/429